BUILT FOR THIS

"Why this time is different."

BUILT FOR
THIS

"Why this time is different."

COPYRIGHT 2023 AARON VICTOR

ALL RIGHTS RESERVED. NO PART OF THIS BOOK MAY BE REPRODUCED, STORED IN A RETRIEVAL SYSTEM, OR TRANSMITTED IN ANY FORM OR BY ANY MEANS, ELECTRONIC, MECHANICAL, PHOTOCOPYING, RECORDING, OR OTHERWISE, EXCEPT FOR BRIEF QUOTATIONS IN CRITICAL REVIEWS OR ARTICLES, WITHOUT THE PRIOR WRITTEN PERMISSION OF THE PUBLISHER.

PUBLISHED BY: AARON VICTOR

COVER DESIGNED BY: DEZINBIZ

Dedicated To

Milton Goodson
1942-2006

One of the greatest men I have ever known.

"There is no greater love than to lay down one's life for one's friends."
John 15:13 NLT

CONTENTS

Dedication i

Foreword iv

Words From Aaron Victor vi

Part 1: "Self-Talk" 1

Day 1 – 5

Part 2: "Perspective" 13

Day 6 – 10

Part 3: "Self-Image" 25

Day 11 – 15

Part 4: "Courage" 37

Day 16 – 20

Part 5: "Boundaries" 49

Day 21 – 25

Part 6: "Consistency" 61

Day 26 – 30

N.EX.T. Steps Required 73

About the Author 77

FOREWORD

Built for this is a 30-day experience to see what is inside you. This devotional is not a magic bullet but the beginning stages of an apprenticeship. Over 30 days, you will get out of this devotional what you put into it. The Built for this 30-day devotional gifts you habits of formation to cultivate a new you. Apprentice and become the person you want to be.

Do not be held hostage by the person your story and origin story may say you should be. You are courageous, daring, hopeful, enduring, bold, fruitful, radiant, and glorious; some haven't cultivated that reality.

Aaron's uncanny hope in people is infectious. If you are reading this, I ask you to trust what is put before you. Trust that each step is for cultivating, as a farmer would the ground to produce fruit. Hence, Aaron believes there is a fruit that can come from you that you will wonder at its harvest.

You are built for this because God does not make mistakes in bringing people into this world or you to this moment. Become the apprentice to something new. Here is to Aaron and 30 days to fresh fruit.

~ Adam "Lumkile" Thomason

Words From Aaron

I believe this journey will change your life significantly. Be grateful for the moments that have brought you to today and know that each one happened for a reason. The feeling inside of you telling you there is more to life than what you are currently experiencing--don't try to ignore it. Embrace it.

You're probably questioning whether or not you have what it takes to get the job done. But think about those around you--do they seem concerned with the things that keep you up at night? Do they feel a desire to change their world for themselves and others? You know the answer is "no," which confuses you because, based on their qualifications, talent, and resources, they could do it too if they just understood.

Instead of convincing others, have faith in yourself. Have the same attitude as David, a shepherd boy who one day became a great leader. Prior to that lunch delivering moment, his time spent with the sheep didn't make sense. But everything changed with one act of courage.

Upon David's confrontation with Goliath, he notice that nobody else was capable or willing to take on the Philistine. He realized that it was his job to put an end the giant's terrorizing of Israel.

David quickly realized that he was the only one who could kill the giant, and even when King Saul offered to give him the king's armor, David knew he had to do it in his own way--the same way he'd done it before while protecting the sheep from lions and bears.

See, David was trained in fields away from people where no one could see him. You have been developed similarly too, but instead of fields you've learned in the darkness of shadows away from opinions and fears of others. You are stronger than you think and can do more than you realize. right now is your time to shine. You have the power to change someone's life for the better.

Here's what to expect over the next 30 days.

Every day, you will come across a quote, each quote is designed for you to reflect, unpack and process. Take some time out of your day - at least 30 minutes - to read the quote, reflection on the insight given for each quote and answer each question thoughtfully. Don't just rush ahead; it's important that you take at least 24 hours to reflect upon your answers and each question so that you can apply it in your own life.

30 minutes a day for 30 days of self-care? Are you worth it? Yes it's worth it, and yes you are worth it. The obstacles that normally stop us no longer stand in our way; instead, the path is laid out before you. You are capable of this journey - resilient enough to fight against what has been thrown at you, strong enough to keep going forward despite all odds...you're built for exactly this!

Part 1

"SELF TALK"

"SELF TALK"

DAY 1

"See change as an asset not as an adversary."

INSIGHT

CHANGE CAN BE AN UNCOMFORTABLE AND DIFFICULT PROCESS, BUT IT IS ESSENTIAL IF WE WANT TO STAY RELEVANT AND IMPACTFUL. IF WE RESIST CHANGE AND IMPROVEMENT, OR SIMPLY TRY TO STAY IN THE SAME PLACE THAT WE'RE ALREADY IN, THEN WE RUN THE RISK OF BECOMING OBSOLETE AND ONLY LIVING IN THE PAST. WHILE IT MAY NOT ALWAYS BE EASY, EMBRACING CHANGE CAN HELP US KEEP UP WITH THE TIMES AND REMAIN A SIGNIFICANT PART OF OUR OWN LIVES AND THOSE AROUND US. CHANGE IS OUR FRIEND —IT'S AN ALLY THAT CAN SHOW US WHAT IS POSSIBLE, GIVING US NEW OPPORTUNITIES FOR GROWTH AND SUCCESS. SO DON'T BE AFRAID TO TAKE ON CHANGE AND USE IT TO YOUR ADVANTAGE—YOU'LL FIND THAT YOU HAVE A LOT MORE POTENTIAL THAN YOU THINK.

WHAT DO YOU DISLIKE THE MOST ABOUT CHANGE?

_____

_____

_____

_____

_____

HOW DO YOU PREPARE FOR CHANGE?

_____

_____

_____

_____

_____

"SELF TALK"

_____

_____
_____
_____
_____
_____
_____
_____
_____
_____
_____
_____
_____
_____
_____
_____
_____
_____
_____
_____
_____

"SELF TALK"

"SELF TALK"

DAY 2

> "Your feelings are real, but the conclusions you make are a choice."

INSIGHT

EMBRACING OUR EMOTIONS CAN BE AN INCREDIBLY POWERFUL TOOL FOR GAINING INSIGHT INTO WHO WE TRULY ARE, OUR VALUES, AND OUR MOTIVATIONS. HOWEVER, IT IS IMPORTANT TO REMEMBER THAT JUST BECAUSE WE FEEL A CERTAIN WAY DOES NOT MEAN IT IS THE ABSOLUTE TRUTH. IT IS ESSENTIAL TO LOOK OBJECTIVELY AT THE FACTS TO ARRIVE AT THE MOST APPROPRIATE CONCLUSION. OUR FEELINGS MAY NOT ALWAYS REFLECT REALITY. BY TAKING BOTH SUBJECTIVE AND OBJECTIVE INFORMATION INTO ACCOUNT, WE CAN MAKE MORE INFORMED DECISIONS THAT BETTER ALIGN WITH OUR AUTHENTIC SELVES.

WHAT CONCLUSIONS HAVE YOU MADE SOLELY BASED ON YOUR FEELINGS?

_____
_____
_____
_____

HOW LONG DO YOU TAKE TO PROCESS YOUR EMOTIONS BEFORE MOVING ON?

_____
_____
_____
_____

"SELF TALK"

"SELF TALK"

DAY 3

"Talk to yourself and stop listening to yourself."

INSIGHT

ONCE WE BECOME MORE AWARE OF THE NEGATIVE THOUGHTS AND MESSAGES THAT ARE SWIRLING AROUND IN OUR MINDS, IT'S IMPORTANT TO TRY TO COUNTERACT THEM WITH POSITIVE ONES. INSTEAD OF THINKING "I CAN'T DO THIS," MAKE A CONSCIOUS EFFORT TO TELL YOURSELF "I WILL TRY MY BEST." TAKING CONTROL OF THESE PESSIMISTIC IDEAS THAT PLAGUE US IS KEY TO SUCCESS AND CAN BE EASILY DONE BY REPLACING THEM WITH MORE ENCOURAGING WORDS. DOING SO HELPS US TO SHAPE OUR OUTLOOK AND ULTIMATELY ALLOWS US TO TAKE OWNERSHIP OF OUR ACTIONS AND OUTCOMES.

WHAT ENCOURAGING MESSAGES DO YOU SAY TO YOURSELF DAILY?

_____
_____
_____
_____
_____

WHAT NEGATIVE MESSAGES DO YOU SAY TO YOURSELF DAILY?

_____
_____
_____
_____
_____

"SELF TALK"

"SELF TALK"

DAY 4

"Intentions and actions must be aligned for positive impact."

INSIGHT

IT CAN BE EASY TO BELIEVE THAT HAVING GOOD INTENTIONS IS ENOUGH FOR SOMETHING TO TURN OUT POSITIVELY. UNFORTUNATELY, THIS IS NOT ALWAYS THE CASE AND IT'S IMPORTANT TO REMEMBER THAT ACTIONS SPEAK LOUDER THAN WORDS. IF YOU WANT YOUR INTENTIONS TO TRULY BE HEARD AND UNDERSTOOD, IT'S NECESSARY TO TAKE THE STEPS THAT WILL MAKE YOUR GOALS A REALITY. WORKING HARD AND STAYING COMMITTED WILL PROVE FAR MORE SUCCESSFUL THAN SIMPLY HOPING FOR THE BEST IN ANY GIVEN SITUATION. SO, IF YOU NEED HELP ACHIEVING SOMETHING POSITIVE, REMEMBER THAT TAKING THE RIGHT STEPS WILL ENSURE THAT YOUR INTENTIONS COME THROUGH IN A POWERFUL WAY.

DOES YOUR PLAN TODAY ALIGN WITH THE INTENTIONS FOR YOUR LIFE? (EXPLAIN)

_____
_____
_____
_____
_____
_____

WHAT DO YOU DO TO BRING YOURSELF INTO ALIGNMENT?

_____
_____
_____
_____
_____
_____

"SELF TALK"

"SELF TALK"

DAY 5

"Without hope you substitute expectations for cynicism and settle for what you have."

INSIGHT

HOPE IS SOMETHING THAT CAN ONLY EXIST WHEN YOU BELIEVE THAT THINGS CAN BE BETTER AND HAVE FAITH IN A GOOD OUTCOME. WHEN HOPE IS CULTIVATED, IT HAS THE POTENTIAL TO LEAD TO AMAZING THINGS. IT CAN HELP PEOPLE TAKE ON CHALLENGING TASKS AND BUILD TOWARD SUCCESS DESPITE ANY OBSTACLES THEY MAY FACE. HOPE SPARKS COURAGE, ENCOURAGES HARD WORK, AND GIVES THE STRENGTH TO STRIVE FOR BIGGER GOALS. AND WHILE HOPE MAY NOT GUARANTEE ANY PARTICULAR RESULT, IT WILL GIVE YOU THE BELIEF THAT NO MATTER WHAT HAPPENS, SOMETHING BETTER IS POSSIBLE. SO, IF THERE'S SOMETHING YOU WANT TO ACCOMPLISH, DON'T FORGET TO TAP INTO YOUR INNER HOPE FOR A FAVORABLE OUTCOME ALONG THE WAY.

WHAT IN YOUR LIFE HAVE YOU SETTLED FOR?

_____
_____
_____
_____
_____
_____

WHAT IS THE THING YOU WANT TO BELIEVE IN AGAIN BUT ARE AFRAID OF BEING DISAPPOINTED?

_____
_____
_____
_____
_____
_____

"SELF TALK"

_____

_____

_____

_____

_____

_____

_____

_____

_____

_____

_____

_____

_____

_____

_____

_____

_____

_____

_____

Part 2

"PERSPECTIVE"

"PERSPECTIVE"

DAY 6

> "Getting better doesn't mean you weren't already good."

INSIGHT

FOR MANY PEOPLE TODAY, THE IDEA OF IMPROVING ON THEIR CURRENT SITUATION IS MET WITH RESISTANCE. THIS MIGHT BE DUE TO FEELING LIKE PROGRESS IS IN SOME WAY A PERSONAL REFLECTION OR CRITICISM, OR IT COULD JUST BE THAT THEY ARE COMFORTABLE AND DON'T FEEL LIKE STRAYING FROM WHAT IS FAMILIAR. WHATEVER THE REASONS, IT'S UNDERSTANDABLE WHY PEOPLE MIGHT HOLD BACK ON DOING SOMETHING THAT MIGHT TAKE THEM OUT OF THEIR COMFORT ZONE. THAT BEING SAID, TAKING RISKS CAN YIELD POSITIVE RESULTS AND ULTIMATELY MAKE THEM BETTER OFF THAN BEFORE, SO IT'S OFTEN WORTH PUSHING PAST THOSE RESERVATIONS FOR THE SAKE OF POTENTIAL GROWTH.

HOW DO YOU VIEW CHANGE?

_____
_____
_____
_____
_____

IS CHANGE IMPROVEMENT OR CONVICTION? (WHY?)

_____
_____
_____
_____
_____

"PERSPECTIVE"

"PERSPECTIVE"

DAY 7

"A plan with imperfections can produce greatness."

INSIGHT

IT'S EASY TO GET CAUGHT UP IN THE ALL-IMPORTANT TASK OF PERFECTING YOUR PLAN BEFORE YOU TAKE ANY ACTION. HOWEVER, IT'S IMPORTANT TO REMEMBER THAT EVEN THE MOST SUCCESSFUL ENTREPRENEURS HAVE SOMETIMES TAKEN RISKS EVEN WHEN THEY WEREN'T QUITE SURE HOW EVERYTHING WOULD TURN OUT. A PRIME EXAMPLE OF THIS IS STEVE JOBS AND THE LAUNCH OF THE ORIGINAL IPHONE. DESPITE KNOWING THAT THE EXISTING NETWORK CAPABILITIES COULDN'T SUPPORT HIS PRODUCT, HE WENT AHEAD WITH IT ANYWAY AND CHANGED THE LANDSCAPE FOREVER. SO NEXT TIME YOU FIND YOURSELF STRUGGLING TO FIND THAT PERFECT PLAN, REMEMBER THAT SOMETIMES TAKING A LEAP DESPITE UNCERTAINTY CAN BE JUST AS IMPORTANT AS NAILING EACH DETAIL DOWN BEFOREHAND.

WHAT'S MOST NECESSARY FOR YOU TO START ON A JOURNEY?

_____
_____
_____
_____
_____
_____

THINK OF THE LAST TIME YOU WERE SUCCESSFUL. WAS THE PLAN PERFECT? (EXPLAIN)

_____
_____
_____
_____
_____
_____

"PERSPECTIVE"

"PERSPECTIVE"

DAY 8

"You cannot gain clarity standing in the same spot."

INSIGHT

MANY OF US STRUGGLE WITH A NEED FOR CONTROL AND CERTAINTY WHEN IT COMES TO MAKING DECISIONS. HOWEVER, WHEN IT COMES TO ACHIEVING SUCCESS, OFTEN THE DETAILS CAN ONLY BE REVEALED BY TAKING ACTION AND GETTING STARTED. THIS CAN BE QUITE INTIMIDATING, PARTICULARLY IF YOU ARE APPROACHING SOMETHING NEW — BUT HAVE NO FEAR. IF WE LOOK BACK ON OUR JOURNEY THUS FAR WE WILL SEE THAT COURAGE, FLEXIBILITY AND RESILIENCE HAVE BEEN OUR GREATEST TEACHERS IN THE UNKNOWN. SO DON'T LET YOURSELF BE HELD BACK BY THE UNCERTAINTY OF NOT KNOWING ALL THE DETAILS UPFRONT — TRUST THAT ONCE YOU TAKE THE FIRST STEP FORWARD YOUR KNOWLEDGE AND UNDERSTANDING WILL INCREASE. WELCOME THE CHALLENGE AND TAKE THE LEAP; YOU MAY JUST SURPRISE YOURSELF WITH WHAT YOU LEARN ALONG THE WAY!

WHAT DO YOU NEED TO SEE TO MOVE FORWARD?

_____
_____
_____
_____
_____

WHAT'S HOLDING YOU BACK?

_____
_____
_____
_____
_____

"PERSPECTIVE"

"PERSPECTIVE"

DAY 9

"Faith allows for one to move toward a vision not yet realized."

INSIGHT

WHAT WE WORK TOWARD DAILY SPEAKS VOLUMES ABOUT OUR DEEPEST VALUES AND WHERE WE HAVE PLACED OUR FAITH. IF WE PAUSE TO ANALYZE OUR DAILY ACTIONS, BOTH BIG AND SMALL, IT IS POSSIBLE TO GAIN INSIGHT INTO THE THINGS WE HOLD NEAR AND DEAR. FOR EXAMPLE, IF YOU SPEND YOUR DAYS FURTHERING EDUCATION OR HELPING OTHERS, THESE MAY BE INDICATORS OF WHERE YOUR TRUST LIES. OUR ACTIONS OFTEN GIVE AWAY MORE THAN WE REALIZE, MAKING REFLECTION AND ANALYSIS OF THESE RECURRING PRACTICES A VALUABLE EXERCISE IN DETERMINING WHAT MATTERS MOST AND HOW FAR OUR FAITH WILL TAKE US.

WHAT IS THE VISION YOU SEE IN YOUR MIND?

_____
_____
_____
_____
_____

WHAT ON YOUR CALENDAR TODAY HAS YOU MOVING TOWARD THE VISION TODAY?

_____
_____
_____
_____
_____

"PERSPECTIVE"

"PERSPECTIVE"

DAY 10

"Your perspective determines whether you see a starting point or a deficit."

INSIGHT

PERSPECTIVE CAN BE A POWERFUL TOOL FOR ACHIEVING SUCCESS, AS IT PROVIDES THE FRAMEWORK TO SEE PROBLEMS AS POSSIBILITIES AND OBSTACLES AS OPPORTUNITIES. BY LOOKING AT CHALLENGES FROM A DIFFERENT ANGLE, WE OPEN OUR MINDS TO CREATIVE RESOLUTIONS AND INNOVATIVE SOLUTIONS THAT MAY NOT HAVE BEEN VISIBLE BEFORE. WITH THIS NEWFOUND PERSPECTIVE, IT BECOMES EASIER TO BREAK THROUGH BOUNDARIES AND TAKE ON HARDSHIPS WITH RENEWED HOPE. IT IS IN THESE MOMENTS WHEN WE COME TO REALIZE THAT WITH THE RIGHT ATTITUDE EVEN THE MOST SEEMINGLY INSURMOUNTABLE ISSUES CAN GIVE WAY TO AN ABUNDANCE OF POTENTIAL.

WHAT IS THE BENEFIT OF WHERE YOU START FROM TODAY?

_____
_____
_____
_____
_____

DESCRIBE THE COMPLETION OF YOUR BEST-CASE SCENARIO?

_____
_____
_____
_____
_____

"PERSPECTIVE"

Part 3

"SELF IMAGE"

"SELF IMAGE"

DAY 11

"Giving your best is not a condition of the moment, it's a reflection of your character."

INSIGHT

WAITING FOR THE PERFECT TIME AND CONDITIONS TO GIVE YOUR BEST IS NOT ONLY UNWISE, BUT IT ALSO REVEALS A SELFISH HEART. IT TELLS THOSE AROUND US THAT THEY DON'T DESERVE OUR FULL EFFORT, NO MATTER WHAT THEY MAY DO OR SAY. FURTHERMORE, THIS MINDSET CAN LEAD US TO MISS OUT ON VALUABLE LEARNING EXPERIENCES, AS WELL AS SHORTCHANGE OUR OWN POTENTIAL AND GROWTH. SUCCESS IS OFTEN ACHIEVED IN THE FACE OF ADVERSITY AND WHEN WE TAKE RISKS. SO INSTEAD OF WAITING FOR EVERYTHING TO BE JUST RIGHT, HAVE THE COURAGE TO GIVE YOUR BEST EVEN IN DIFFICULT SITUATIONS—YOU WILL BE SURPRISED BY HOW FAR YOU CAN GO!

WHAT DO THE PEOPLE AROUND SAY ABOUT YOUR CHARACTER?

_____
_____
_____
_____
_____

WHAT ARE THE CONDITIONS WITHIN WHICH YOU THRIVE?

_____
_____
_____
_____
_____

"SELF IMAGE"

"SELF IMAGE"

DAY 12

> "Belief can unlock possibilities or create limitations."

INSIGHT

OUR VIEWPOINT OF THE WORLD IS INTIMATELY CONNECTED TO WHAT WE BELIEVE. WHEN WE TAKE INSPIRED ACTION AND MOVE FORWARD WITH AN OPEN HEART, ALL KINDS OF WONDERFUL POSSIBILITIES UNFOLD BEFORE US. THOUGH THE JOURNEY MAY BE CHALLENGING AT TIMES, REMEMBER THAT GREATER LESSONS LIE AHEAD IF YOU CAN STAY TRUE TO YOUR VISION AND KEEP BELIEVING IN YOURSELF. THE COURAGE TO CHOOSE FAITH OVER FEAR WILL GUIDE YOU THROUGH ANY SITUATION — ALLOWING YOU TO EVENTUALLY REACH THE DESTINATION YOU DESIRED FOR YOURSELF.

WHAT DO YOU SEE FOR YOUR LIFE WHEN YOU WAKE UP IN THE MORNING?

_____
_____
_____
_____
_____

WHAT ARE YOU HOPING FOR IN THIS MOMENT OF YOUR LIFE?

_____
_____
_____
_____
_____

"SELF IMAGE"

"SELF IMAGE"

DAY 13

"Comfort settles one into apathy and removes passion and motivation."

INSIGHT

IT'S EASY TO GET COMFORTABLE WHEN LIFE IS GOING SMOOTHLY. BUT IT IS PRECISELY THIS COMPLACENCY THAT PREVENTS US FROM ACHIEVING TRUE EXCELLENCE. IT'S IMPORTANT TO REMEMBER THAT GREATNESS REQUIRES EFFORT AND DEDICATION, AND OFTEN MEANS STEPPING OUT OF OUR COMFORT ZONES. WHEN THINGS START FEELING TOO FAMILIAR, BE AWARE OF YOUR COMPLACENCY — IT IS THE NATURAL ENEMY OF EXCELLENCE. ONLY THROUGH PURSUING GREATNESS AND PUSHING OURSELVES FURTHER CAN WE REACH HEIGHTS BEYOND WHAT WE THOUGHT POSSIBLE. BE BRAVE, TAKE RISKS, AND ALWAYS STRIVE FOR SOMETHING GREATER THAN COMFORT — THAT'S WHERE TRUE GREATNESS LIES!

WHAT IN YOUR LIFE HAS YOU THE MOST COMFORTABLE?

_____
_____
_____
_____
_____

WHICH ONE HAS MORE INFLUENCE, YOUR MOTIVATION OR COMFORT? (WHY?)

_____
_____
_____
_____
_____

"SELF IMAGE"

"SELF IMAGE"

DAY 14

"Normalized greatness creates unvalued experiences."

INSIGHT

IT IS EASY TO GET STUCK IN OUR COMFORT ZONE AND BECOME OBLIVIOUS TO THE UNIQUE GIFTS AND TALENTS THAT WE EACH POSSESS. JUST BECAUSE SOMETHING IS "NORMAL" OR MUNDANE TO US, DOESN'T MEAN IT ISN'T GREAT OR VALUABLE TO OTHERS. IN MANY WAYS, THE THINGS THAT ARE SPECIAL AND DIFFERENT ABOUT US CAN BE WHAT SETS US APART FROM THE CROWD AND MAKE US TRULY VALUABLE IN OUR OWN UNIQUE WAY. CELEBRATE AND SHARE YOUR DIFFERENCES; YOU NEVER KNOW WHO MIGHT APPRECIATE THEM!

IN YOUR OPINION WHAT IS GREAT?

_____
_____
_____
_____
_____

WHAT DO YOU DISMISS AS I WAS "DOING WHAT I HAD TO DO"?

_____
_____
_____
_____
_____

"SELF IMAGE"

_____

_____

_____

_____

_____

_____

_____

_____

_____

_____

_____

_____

_____

_____

_____

_____

_____

_____

_____

"SELF IMAGE"

DAY 15

"What's behind you prepared you for what's in front of you."

INSIGHT

LIFE CAN BE UNPREDICTABLE, BUT EVERYTHING THAT WE HAVE EXPERIENCED HAS HELPED TO SHAPE WHO WE ARE AND PREPARE US FOR WHAT IS TO COME. EVERY TEAR SHED, EVERY MISTAKE MADE, AND EVERY CHALLENGE FACED HAS SERVED A HIGHER PURPOSE, EVEN IF IT'S NOT ALWAYS IMMEDIATELY APPARENT. WE SHOULD TAKE COMFORT IN KNOWING THAT NOTHING HAS BEEN WASTED; EACH OF THESE EXPERIENCES HAVE BROUGHT US CLOSER TO OUR GOALS AND THE OPPORTUNITIES AWAITING US IN THE PRESENT MOMENT. WITH THIS UNDERSTANDING, WE CAN FACE EACH DAY WITH COURAGE AND CONFIDENCE, TRUSTING THAT WE ARE PREPARED FOR WHATEVER COMES OUR WAY.

DESCRIBE A MOMENT WHEN YOU DIDN'T THINK YOU WOULD MAKE IT?

_____
_____
_____
_____
_____
_____

WHAT DID YOU LEARN ABOUT YOURSELF IN THAT PROCESS?

_____
_____
_____
_____
_____
_____

"SELF IMAGE"

"SELF IMAGE"

Part 4

"COURAGE"

"COURAGE"

DAY 16

"Blazing a trail for others takes courage and faith."

INSIGHT

OFTEN, WE CAN BE HELD BACK BY OUR OWN LACK OF COURAGE AND THE FEAR OF FAILURE. BUT IF SOMETHING HAS NEVER BEEN DONE BEFORE, THE ONLY WAY TO DO IT IS TO TAKE THAT FIRST BRAVE STEP. BE THE ONE TO HAVE THE COURAGE TO TRY SOMETHING NEW AND CREATE A PATH WHERE OTHERS CAN FOLLOW. TAKE A CHANCE ON YOURSELF AND DON'T BE AFRAID TO BLAZE YOUR OWN TRAIL—WHO KNOWS WHAT AMAZING THINGS YOU CAN ACCOMPLISH IF YOU JUST HAVE THE CONFIDENCE TO TAKE THAT FIRST STEP! SO DON'T WAIT AROUND FOR SOMEONE ELSE TO DO IT—BE THE ONE WHO TAKES INITIATIVE AND EMBODIES ALL THAT IS POSSIBLE.

WHO BENEFITS WHEN YOU SUCCEED AT WHAT'S IN FRONT OF YOU?

_____
_____
_____
_____
_____

TODAY, WHAT WILL TAKE THE MOST COURAGE TO COMPLETE?

_____
_____
_____
_____
_____

"COURAGE"

"COURAGE"

DAY 17

"Have the courage to rewrite your story."

INSIGHT

FOR MANY, THE IDEA OF TAKING ACTION IN A NEW DIRECTION CAN BE DAUNTING. FEAR OF FAILURE AND DOUBT CAN CRIPPLE OUR AMBITION AND KEEP US FROM LIVING OUR BEST LIVES. BUT IT'S IMPORTANT TO REMEMBER THAT FEAR IS ONLY TEMPORARY AND DOESN'T HAVE TO DEFINE US. TAKING MEANINGFUL STEPS TOWARD SOMETHING NEW — NO MATTER HOW SMALL — CAN BE INCREDIBLY EMPOWERING AND HELP US TAKE CONTROL OF OUR OWN STORY. ULTIMATELY, IT'S THESE CONSISTENT ACTIONS THAT WILL REWRITE OUR STORIES AND CREATE NEW EXPERIENCES. DON'T LET YOUR BAD HABITS OR PAST TRAUMA DEFINE YOU; INSTEAD, USE THEM AS AN OPPORTUNITY TO START SOMETHING FRESH!

WHAT ABOUT YOUR CURRENT STORY DO YOU LIKE?

_____
_____
_____
_____
_____
_____

WHAT ABOUT YOUR CURRENT STORY DO YOU WANT TO CHANGE?

_____
_____
_____
_____
_____
_____

"COURAGE"

"COURAGE"

DAY 18

"Deeds are about what you have; faith is about what you can have."

INSIGHT

BELIEVING IN SOMETHING YOU CAN'T SEE IS A TALL ORDER, BUT THAT'S WHAT FAITH TRULY IS: THE STRENGTH TO BELIEVE IN SOMETHING EVEN WHEN THERE IS NO TANGIBLE PROOF. FAITH DOESN'T JUST COME FROM WITHIN—IT'S COMMUNICATED AND EXPRESSED THROUGH OUR ACTIONS. OUR DESIRE FOR WHAT WE CANNOT YET SEE CREATES A POWERFUL MOTIVATION TO ACT IN WAYS THAT ARE CONGRUENT WITH OUR BELIEFS, ENSURING THE INTEGRITY OF THE VISION WE HAVE FOR OURSELVES AND THE WORLD AROUND US. IT IS HERE, BETWEEN BELIEF AND ACTION, THAT FAITH EXISTS —A BRIDGE CONNECTING US TO OUR DEEPEST DESIRES AND GREATEST POTENTIALS.

ARE YOU MOVING IN FAITH OR LOGIC? (WHY?)

_____
_____
_____
_____
_____

IS WHAT YOU CURRENTLY HAVE THE DREAM YOU HAVE ALWAYS WANTED? (DESCRIBE)

_____
_____
_____
_____
_____
_____

"COURAGE"

"COURAGE"

DAY 19

> "Where you come from is where you find the strength to lead."

INSIGHT

TAKING A STEP BACK AND REFLECTING ON OUR ROOTS CAN OPEN OUR EYES TO THE STRENGTH OF OUR STORY. FROM THE JOURNEY THAT BROUGHT US HERE TO THE PEOPLE WHO HAVE HELPED SHAPE US, THERE IS POTENTIAL IN UNDERSTANDING WHERE WE COME FROM. IT IS THIS HISTORY AND HERITAGE THAT HAS ENABLED US TO REACH OUR GOALS AND DREAMS, PROVIDING US WITH THE SKILLSET WE NEED TO THRIVE AND EXCEL. OUR BACKGROUND IS MORE THAN JUST A SOURCE OF PRIDE, IT IS WHAT MAKES US QUALIFIED TO DO WHAT WE DO. BY EMBRACING THIS NARRATIVE OF GROWTH AND EVOLUTION, WE HONOR OUR UNIQUE IDENTITIES AND CELEBRATE ALL THAT WE'VE ACCOMPLISHED ALONG THE WAY.

HOW DID YOU OVERCOME WHAT YOU WENT THROUGH?

_____
_____
_____
_____
_____

WHAT ARE THE MOST BENEFICIAL LESSONS YOU'VE LEARNED?

_____
_____
_____
_____
_____

"COURAGE"

"COURAGE"

DAY 20

"Your gift was meant to be on full display."

INSIGHT

HIDING IS OFTEN SEEN AS THE EASY WAY OUT OF DIFFICULT SITUATIONS; HOWEVER, IT RARELY PRODUCES DESIRABLE OUTCOMES. INSTEAD, IT ONLY LEADS TO FRUSTRATION AND DISSATISFACTION FOR YOURSELF AND THOSE AROUND YOU. BY AVOIDING ADDRESSING THE ISSUE AT HAND, IT RUNS THE RISK OF LEAVING EVERYONE FEELING UNFULFILLED AND UNAPPRECIATED. IT IS IMPORTANT TO REMEMBER THAT FACING ADVERSITY IS OFTEN NECESSARY TO GROW AND DEVELOP. BY BEING OPEN AND HONEST WITH OURSELVES AND OTHERS, WE CAN FIND A MORE POSITIVE RESOLUTION.

ON A SCALE FROM 1-100, HOW MUCH OF YOUR GIFT IS ON FULL DISPLAY? (DESCRIBE)

_____
_____
_____
_____
_____

WHAT HOLDS YOU BACK FROM BEING ANYTHING LESS THAN 100%?

_____
_____
_____
_____
_____

"COURAGE"

Part 5

"BOUNDARIES"

"BOUNDARIES"

DAY 21

"Fight the need to do everything, everything you can do isn't meant for you to do."

INSIGHT

WE ALL WANT TO PUT OUR BEST FOOT FORWARD AND MAKE SURE THAT WHATEVER WE'RE DOING RECEIVES THE BEST OF US. THAT'S WHY IT'S IMPORTANT TO FOCUS ON WHAT MATTERS MOST TO YOU, BECAUSE THAT IS WHERE YOU NEED PUT YOUR TIME AND EFFORT. EVERYTHING ELSE CAN BE DELEGATED OR DONE BY SOMEONE ELSE — YOU ONLY HAVE SO MUCH ENERGY AND ATTENTION TO GIVE, SO IT'S IMPORTANT TO PRIORITIZE ACCORDINGLY. BY DEDICATING YOURSELF ONLY TO WHAT TRULY MATTERS, YOU'LL BE ABLE TO MAKE A GREATER IMPACT IN THE LONG RUN, RATHER THAN SPREADING YOURSELF TOO THIN TRYING TO DO IT ALL. SO, TAKE THE TIME TO REFLECT ON WHAT'S MOST IMPORTANT AND GIVE THOSE THINGS YOUR UNDIVIDED ATTENTION —EVERYTHING ELSE WILL NATURALLY FALL INTO PLACE.

WHAT HAPPENED THE LAST TIME YOU GAVE SOMEONE CONTROL?

_____
_____
_____
_____
_____
_____

WHAT DO YOU DO WELL THAT NEEDS MORE OF YOUR ATTENTION?

_____
_____
_____
_____
_____
_____

"BOUNDARIES"

"BOUNDARIES"

DAY 22

"Be careful, the viewpoints of other people can and will limit the viewpoint of yourself."

INSIGHT

BY TAKING THE TIME TO LISTEN TO AND CONSIDER DIFFERENT PERSPECTIVES, WE CAN MAKE MORE THOUGHTFUL AND INFORMED DECISIONS THAT ARE BENEFICIAL NOT JUST FOR US, BUT ALSO THOSE AROUND US. RATHER THAN MAKING DECISIONS BASED ON OUR OWN POINT OF VIEW, WE CAN USE THE VIEWPOINTS OF OTHERS AS A TOOL TO HELP GUIDE OUR CHOICES. THIS APPROACH ALLOWS US TO BETTER EVALUATE THE POTENTIAL CONSEQUENCES THAT OUR DECISIONS MIGHT HAVE BEFORE MAKING A FINAL CALL. WHEN DONE RIGHT, THIS CAN CREATE SOLUTIONS THAT SATISFY EVERYONE, RESULTING IN COLLECTIVE GROWTH AND SUCCESS.

HOW DO YOU FEEL ABOUT THE OPINIONS OF OTHERS?

_____
_____
_____
_____
_____

DESCRIBE HOW DO YOU SEE YOURSELF. WHAT IS YOUR SELF-IMAGE?

_____
_____
_____
_____
_____

"BOUNDARIES"

"BOUNDARIES"

DAY 23

"Discipline is the boundary where your feelings need to reside."

INSIGHT

OUR FEELINGS DO NOT DETERMINE THE OUTCOME OF OUR LIVES, BUT INSTEAD IT IS THE CONSISTENT CHOICES AND HABITS WE ENGAGE IN THAT SHAPE OUR OUTCOMES. WE ALL REALIZE MOMENTS WHEN WE FEEL OVERWHELMED OR UNCERTAIN, AND IT IS IMPORTANT TO SEPARATE THESE FEELINGS FROM WHAT SHOULD BE DONE. INSTEAD OF LETTING EMOTIONS DRIVE OUR DECISIONS, WE MUST COMMIT TO STEADILY MAKING CHOICES BASED ON OUR VALUES AND GOALS. DOING SO WILL ENSURE THAT WE STAY ON A PATH TOWARD SUCCESS AND SATISFACTION DESPITE DIFFICULT CIRCUMSTANCES.

WHAT'S YOUR INITIAL REACTION WHEN YOU HEAR THE WORD "DISCIPLINE"?

___

___

___

___

___

HOW MANY TIMES A WEEK DO YOU NOT MAKE PROGRESS BECAUSE YOU DON'T FEEL LIKE IT?

___

___

___

___

___

"BOUNDARIES"

"BOUNDARIES"

DAY 24

"You are only distracted when the commitment gets lost in the process."

INSIGHT

WE OFTEN GET SO CAUGHT UP IN BEING BUSY THAT WE FORGET TO BE PRODUCTIVE. IT CAN SEEM AS IF OUR LIVES ARE FILLED WITH TASKS AND RESPONSIBILITIES AND THERE IS NO END IN SIGHT; BUT IT'S IMPORTANT TO REMEMBER THAT SOMETIMES BEING PRODUCTIVE IS MORE ABOUT BEING EFFICIENT THAN FILLING OUR DAYS. INSTEAD OF TAKING ON A MILLION TASKS AT ONCE, TAKE A STEP BACK AND FOCUS ON WHAT WILL MAKE US MOST PRODUCTIVE IN ACHIEVING OUR GOALS. LEARNING HOW TO PRIORITIZE AND MANAGE OUR TIME EFFECTIVELY CAN GIVE US THE SPACE WE NEED TO FOCUS ON WHAT'S IMPORTANT FOR OURSELVES AND FOR OTHERS.

WHY DID YOU GET STARTED?

_____
_____
_____
_____
_____

WHAT ONE THING DO YOU NEED TO FOCUS ON TODAY TO CONTINUE?

_____
_____
_____
_____
_____
_____

"BOUNDARIES"

"BOUNDARIES"

DAY 25

"There is beauty in the moment, don't miss the beauty focusing too far into the future."

INSIGHT

OUR PRESENT MOMENTS DETERMINE OUR FUTURE LIVES, SO IT IS IMPORTANT TO BE MINDFUL OF HOW WE USE OUR TIME NOW. IF WE WORK HARD IN THE PRESENT AND MAKE CONSCIOUS DECISIONS THAT ALIGN WITH OUR DESIRED FUTURE OUTCOMES, THEN WE WILL BE ABLE TO ENJOY THE FRUITS OF OUR LABOR LATER. SO, LET'S NOT FORGET THAT LIFE IS LIVED IN THE MOMENT — OUR CURRENT ACTIONS SHAPE OUR FUTURE LIVES. TAKE A MOMENT TO FOCUS ON YOUR GOALS AND DREAMS; WORKING NOW COULD CREATE A MUCH BRIGHTER AND MORE DESIRABLE FUTURE.

WHAT'S THE BEAUTY OF THIS MOMENT IN YOUR LIFE?

_____
_____
_____
_____
_____

WHAT MOMENTS HAVE YOU MISSED IN FRONT OF YOU FOCUSING ON THE FUTURE? (KIDS, FAMILY, ETC.)

_____
_____
_____
_____
_____

"BOUNDARIES"

Part 6

"CONSISTENCY"

"CONSISTENCY"

DAY 26

"Improving on greatness is how excellence is sustained."

INSIGHT

SUCCESS CAN BE AN ENEMY TO GREATNESS IF WE BECOME COMPLACENT OR DON'T CONTINUE TO STRIVE FORWARD. IT'S EASY TO REST ON OUR LAURELS AND LIVE IN THE PAST, BUT THAT WILL LIMIT OUR POTENTIAL AND PREVENT US FROM ACHIEVING TRUE GREATNESS. WE MUST CONSTANTLY CHALLENGE OURSELVES AND MOVE BEYOND THE SUCCESS OF YESTERDAY IF WE WANT TO CREATE A BETTER TOMORROW. DON'T LET YOURSELF GIVE INTO FEAR AND AVOID TAKING NEW RISKS — INSTEAD, USE THE ACCOMPLISHMENTS OF YOUR PAST AS A STEPPING STONE FOR THE FUTURE. WITH HARD WORK, RESILIENCE, AND DEDICATION, YOU CAN MOVE FORWARD AND CREATE SOMETHING EVEN GREATER THAN BEFORE.

HOW ARE YOU GETTING BETTER TODAY?

___

___

___

___

___

WHAT IS THE LEVEL OF SUCCESS YOU DESIRE IN YOUR LIFE?

___

___

___

___

___

"CONSISTENCY"

"CONSISTENCY"

DAY 27

"The journey goes through a process."

INSIGHT

ACHIEVING SUCCESS AND CREATING SOMETHING TRULY MEANINGFUL TAKES TIME AND EFFORT — IT'S RARELY SOMETHING THAT CAN BE ACCOMPLISHED OVERNIGHT. DESPITE THE INITIAL EXCITEMENT, MANY OF US FIND OURSELVES LOSING SIGHT OF OUR PROMISE AS WE TRUDGE THROUGH THE PROCESS. DON'T LET THIS HAPPEN TO YOU — STAY FOCUSED ON YOUR VISION AND REMEMBER WHY YOU STARTED IN THE FIRST PLACE. THOUGH SUCCESS MAY NOT BE IMMEDIATE, PROGRESS IS STILL BEING MADE — CELEBRATE EACH SMALL STEP FORWARD AND TRUST THAT IN DUE TIME ALL YOUR HARD WORK WILL PAY OFF! NO MATTER HOW LONG IT TAKES, NEVER FORGET YOUR PROMISE, AND KEEP GOING — GREAT THINGS TAKE TIME!

WHICH ONE SCARES YOUR MORE, THE JOURNEY OR THE PROCESS? (WHY?)

_____
_____
_____
_____
_____
_____

WHAT IS WORTH GOING THROUGH THE PROCESS OF COMPLETION?

_____
_____
_____
_____
_____
_____

"CONSISTENCY"

"CONSISTENCY"

DAY 28

"The world needs you to show up."

INSIGHT

WE OFTEN FIND OURSELVES UNDERESTIMATING THE POWER OF OUR OWN BELIEFS AND EXPERIENCES. WHAT WE MAY SEE AS INSIGNIFICANT COULD HAVE A TREMENDOUSLY POSITIVE EFFECT ON ANOTHER PERSON. WHAT WE BELIEVE ISN'T VALUABLE IS OFTEN EXACTLY WHAT SOMEONE ELSE IS LOOKING FOR — THEY JUST HAVEN'T DISCOVERED IT YET. WE CAN BE A SOURCE OF WISDOM AND COMFORT TO THOSE IN NEED; SOMETIMES THE VERY THING THAT WE'VE TAKEN FOR GRANTED IS THE VERY THING THEY ARE SEARCHING FOR. OUR UNIQUE PERSPECTIVE CAN CHANGE LIVES, SO DON'T BE AFRAID TO SHARE YOUR EXPERIENCES AND IDEAS WITH OTHERS — YOU NEVER KNOW WHO MIGHT BENEFIT FROM YOUR INSIGHTS!

WHAT INCIDENT TAUGHT YOU THAT SHOWING UP IS DANGEROUS?

_____
_____
_____
_____
_____

HOW DOES IT FEEL TO KNOW YOU'RE THE ANSWER TO SOMEONE'S PRAYERS? (WHY?)

_____
_____
_____
_____
_____

"CONSISTENCY"

"CONSISTENCY"

DAY 29

"Consistency of behaviors over time is stewardship of freedom."

INSIGHT

OUR DAILY ACTIONS REVEAL HOW WE HAVE STEWARDED OUR GIFTS, AND WHEN USED PROPERLY, OUR ACTIONS ALSO BECOME A SIGN OF GRATITUDE. WHETHER IT'S DEDICATING OURSELVES TO CREATING SOMETHING MEANINGFUL OR HELPING OTHERS IN NEED, OUR LIVES CAN BECOME A LIVING PRAYER OF THANKSGIVING. EVERY SMALL ACT PERFORMED WITH LOVE AND CARE SPEAKS VOLUMES ABOUT HOW MUCH WE APPRECIATE THE OPPORTUNITIES GIVEN TO US. IT IS THROUGH OUR DAILY EFFORTS THAT WE DEMONSTRATE GRATITUDE TO THOSE AROUND US BY SHOWING THEM HOW OUR BLESSINGS ARE BEING PUT TO GOOD USE. BY DOING SO, WE MAKE THE WORLD A BETTER PLACE WHILE HONORING THE GRACE BESTOWED UPON US.

IF ACTIONS SPEAK LOUDER THAN WORDS, WHAT DO YOUR ACTIONS SAY ABOUT YOU RIGHT NOW?

_____
_____
_____
_____
_____
_____

WHAT BEHAVIORS DO YOU WANT TO BE CONSISTENT? (WHY?)

_____
_____
_____
_____
_____
_____

"CONSISTENCY"

"CONSISTENCY"

DAY 30

"Consistency is showing up even when the desired result is not present."

INSIGHT

TRUST CAN BE HARD TO COME BY, ESPECIALLY WHEN WE FEEL LIKE WE CONSTANTLY NEED TO PROVE OURSELVES. BUT TRUST IS BUILT AND MAINTAINED THROUGH CONSISTENCY, AND IT STARTS WITH TRUSTING OURSELVES. WHEN OUR ACTIONS ARE CONSISTENT, OTHERS WILL BEGIN TO RECOGNIZE US AS RELIABLE AND TRUSTWORTHY. WE MUST ALSO REMEMBER THAT WHILE TRUST MAY TAKE TIME TO BUILD, IT CAN BE EASILY ERODED BY INCONSISTENCY. AS SUCH, WE MUST REMAIN MINDFUL OF OUR DECISIONS AND STRIVE TO MAINTAIN A LEVEL OF TRUSTWORTHINESS IN ALL ASPECTS OF LIFE. AT THE END OF THE DAY, IF YOU WANT OTHERS TO TRUST YOU, FIRST LEARN HOW TO TRUST YOURSELF.

WHAT'S THE HARDEST PART FOR YOU IN BEING CONSISTENT?

_____
_____
_____
_____
_____

ARE YOU DRIVEN MORE BY THE RESULTS OR THE MASTERY OF THE JOURNEY? (WHY?)

_____
_____
_____
_____
_____

"CONSISTENCY"

N.EX.T Steps Required

Well done on completing this 30 day voyage. With careful consideration and regular work, you are beginning to see yourself in a new light. Every action taken creates more clarity about who you are and the assurance that you have what it takes to take on whatever is ahead of you - and this time will be different. You are different now, and the old story of thinking less of yourself is fading as your confidence grows knowing full well that you are ready for whatever lies ahead.

I encourage you to stay committed to the path you are on and not go back to where you started 30 days ago. Embrace discipline and let it guide your feelings and behavior over time so that the results of your life become more predictable.

Finally, be persistent. Oftentimes, people won't do the difficult work necessary to change because they don't see results right away. However, you've stuck with it for the last 30 days and proven that you're capable of being consistent. This is only the beginning--keep going!

The visions of your mind will be the reality of your life if you take consistent steps in the direction of your goal. Keep going, this time is different because you know you are Built for This!

Join N.E.X.T. Steps Required at:

https://www.lvlthree.com/nextsteps

ABOUT THE AUTHOR

Aaron Victor, is a sought after speaker, leader and award winning coach. With 25 years plus of coaching individuals and organizations across multiple industries and sectors, Aaron is committed to helping you get "it". He knows when you gain clarity on your "it", your life will forever be different.

Aaron is dedicated to helping people achieve success in all areas of their lives. He provides clear and concise direction through strategic planning, goal setting, and action steps. His simple, step-by-step approach removes any excuses that people might use to justify their lack of success.

Aaron is a husband to Ebonique. Brother to Angie and Adam. Son to Victor and Denise. Dad to Chanese, and "Uncle Aaron " to Nate, BJ, Zipporah, Zayne-Baltimore and Zari.

FOLLOW ON INSTAGRAM: @ASKAARONVICTOR

VISIT WEBSITE: WWW.LVLTHREE.COM

Made in the USA
Columbia, SC
21 March 2023

14086355R00055